Veil/Unveil

Susan McCaslin

THE ST. THOMAS POETRY SERIES

CANADIAN CATALOGUING IN PUBLICATION DATA

McCaslin, Susan, 1947 –
   Veil/unveil

(St. Thomas Poetry Series)
Poems.
ISBN 0-9697802-4-9

I. St. Thomas Poetry Series (Association). II. Title. III. Series.

PS8575.C43V44   1997   C811'.54   C97-931639-1
 PR9199.3.M33V44   1997

Some of these poems appeared previously in The New Quarterly, Journal of Feminist Studies in Religion, Contemporary Verse 2, Grain, Vox Feminarum, Literature and Belief, Wascana Review of Contemporary Poetry and Short Fiction, and Bellowing Ark.

Cover wood engraving by Nancy Ruth Jackson,
   hand printed from the original block.
Typeset, printed, & bound by Coach House Printing

The St. Thomas Poetry Series,
c/o St. Thomas's Church,
383 Huron Street,
Toronto, Ontario
M5S 2G5

For Mark and Claire

"When will the repose of the dead come about
  and when will the new world come?"
  He said to them:
"What you expect has come, but you know it not."

The Gospel of Thomas

Contents

In the Apple Tree, Singing

I am seven, perfect age, the age of
fallen, curious Alice, but I climb
rather than fall through the crusty
limbs of the apple

who carries me to her bushy crown,

feeds me rosy tartness in my place,
third row of branches up, my leafy
queenly seat

where I sing higher and higher
faltering coloratura soprano,
hoping secretly the neighbours
will overhear

remark over the fence, "What a
beautiful voice on that girl,
so young. She should go in
for the opera."

Anna's Watch

Was it so yellowed when it graced
the hand of great-grandmother Anna
who scribbled verse, sent me poems

cut from ephemera and church programs?
Sometimes she crafted her own fancy cards,
pasting down letters from home journals

in a mysterious pastiche of salutation.
When I was born she wrote my parents
I would be a blessing, "in children

the light of the world." It sat golden,
solid, on the circle of her wrist
carved with rivering veins.

She who lived so well to 96, counting
minutes by piano hymns, pulse singing,
column of air rising and falling.

If It Does Not Sing, the Heart

sighs deep in its ebony core
ruining the free air
missing connections to Orion,
Aldebaran, Andromeda
(next stop nowhere)
if it does not sing or cry

is an opal oboe concerto
displaced, becomes impertinent
foolish, slips outside itself
making monstrous discord

ends on a kind of voice ladder
where it climbs, gropes and wrestles
rungs ringing the air the whole long night.

Saint Cecilia

Your nimbus is a breakable metallic plate—
space age—but the braided, bundled hair
suggests 18th century rigour—an ode.

If your airborne organ pipes were to resound
past the pristine edges of this card I hold
in my hand where your stillness flickers

unimpaired, would the bedraggled lilies
at your hand erect themselves
against the light and blow?

Wine Dark

Wild and hungry to send messages
or sea music to Neptune,
I am a clear iris rotating in a sphere.

I pretend to be a small uncertain fish
eaten and coughed up like pearls.
I touch the delicate hair of sea spiders
worrying that my words will be lost
in the enormous drift.

I understand nothing
saying, "Hold me in your belly."
I dream of flying past this galaxy
and long to empty myself.

Persephone

Out of the long blocked dark she trails
behind herself, stepping on ash roses
leaving no impression, impressed by little.

All the burgeoning lilacs and lilies
in the upper world are cool trickles
to which she bends her upward ear,

the dark Lord long erased from her brain,
the frenzied mother, frail and far above
her treading. At this halfway house,

gathering herself for the last ascent,
she will ask no one the way, pause
to touch the snail's small cusp,

the spongy sides of the sleepy sheep
who lost its way going down
the dark, dripping, cavernous stair.

She will not rejoin her mother this year
or return to the dark king who scooped
her body up so many turns of the earth.

She will (at the risk of disappointing
or seeming rude) remake her myth
as the seasons rotate without her.

Walking Over My Father's Grave

It is Mother's day and I have abandoned her
density to honour my ghostly father who
used to walk me over family plots singing
"memento mori," and I am intrigued
by rounding green mounds, worn
lettered stone, quiet military urns
drooping chrysanthemums, but his name
does not flare out on any of the stones.

I am sleepwalking, groping through Gethsemane,
Garden of Prayer, quiescence row, rummaging
for his name. I stumble on the convivial
plaques of my grandparents and his
only a few paces further on, appearing
and sinking like the heads of dolphins;
his plate and dates an altar under which
he floats or scrabbles nameless
my father still.

And I am swimming over my father's grave,
ghostly, pale, but luminous, a whale
churning through time where I am turning
sod away on either side and it splashes
seismic up and down the coasts.

I am ferrying myself into my father's house
past the mahogany furniture, the shelves
of curios, and the perfect diamond
in a blue silk box expressly intended
for my mother's hand.

I am a deep-sea diver for that ring,
hauling it back to her through reefs of dreams,
the war-torn lachrymose sea.

Just the Other Night

I saw Jesus, Buddha, and Mohammed
on a tufted slope overlooking a city
which could have been Jerusalem but was not,
sharing a coffee in brown stoneware mugs
they had ground from earth's sweet coffers.

And none of them was preaching or arguing
with the other about anything
because they were tracking the course
of a small black ant struggling
to attain a crest of its choosing.

How to help without interfering
was all their talk,
and admiration of the rich soil
which cupped them all like unbroken shards
against a sea-dropped sky.

For Rilke

This is the only way to live, typing and dreaming
and thinking the future in the present, the past
in the future, the circularity and familiarity of time.

Angels used to dance on pins but here they only
prick their tiny bare feet on shards of brittle glass.
It seems like only tomorrow they blazoned their muscular
pinions in miles of crushed, grappled light,
but now no one in her left mind
wants to risk a tumble.

Jacob paid with a limp, becoming history's lame duck,
and lived to enjoy his fame.

Yet if I risk typing them into nooks of unknowing
and wheeze them as superfluous thoughts
out the top of my head,
no bombs will be exploding
and no harm.

It is only when I remember well they are not
so puny and unhale, but big
with that feeling of enormity I dreamed
as a feverish child, that I wonder
if they should have been summoned so soon
as if they were always waiting.

Who summoned whom? In the divine delirium
let them enter whisking their brooms,
cleaning into every corner, till the cloud
of dust grows nebulous and grand, dropping
its sweet embroidered rain into apophatic hearts.

Just when you think they are done and the
plunging sweetness must sour,

they transit your pen and taunt you
with completed poems you will never write.

Perhaps this is why they come—
to whisper the words and disappear,
so you will write others to suggest them.

This is why you welcome them, wash and kiss
their lovely translucent feet, make a nest
for them in your timebombed flesh
where Love precedes.

Aquarian

Here at the debacle of an age
light slides under the door.
Here in the collapsing culture's
atmosphere of ruin
wakes the unquenched child
who takes the dipper in her fist
and inhales the first buttery drops
of new sun, braces to turn
the zodiacal wheel.

Out of the social collapse,
Aquarian aroma of burning sand—
blazing dancing Christ, Buddha, Mithras,
Shiva, Self, Divine Imagination
what you will, or do not

stained and sinless
versatile and sufficient.

Claritas

You are volatile stone.
I long for your piecemeal
words,
languish in your presence
and absence.

Nothing satisfies.

You carry meanings like clouds
necklaced across a January sky.

I cannot decipher your metaphors,
vague and undulant as Neptune.

I long for a clarity
that undoes me.

Gnosis 1

We are the gnostic heresy
distributing the sacraments,
conducting Christos the first-blown rose

dreaming in beds or rolling in streams
where like underworld sturgeon
there are things we know.

We have been called elitist, secretive,
when the secret is open as glass,
meaning imagination, imaginal closets

cloisters or chambers turned in and out.
The Church called us dualists
(though all we ever said was,

"inner and outer are one,"
or, "the kingdom is laid out like wheat")
just because the revelation continued

and hierarchy wanted to stop it in its tracks,
worship a corpse on a cross who flew
into our bodies and souls not separate

and started table-dancing.
So now the false God, Demiurge,
is technology with a capital T and idolatry

of the machine, but we are inside riding it
like Poe's mechanical chess player, stubbornly
human. And they called us orgiastic

because we chanted the holiness of matter
and its secret urge to rise, just because
we wouldn't have secondhand anything

but sipped heady drops of pure experience
saying, "I don't believe, I know,"
after drawing the vision over the bone

and walking it down the hall, feeling
down the toes and nostrils the aroma
of holiness which is wholeness where

the elastic soul gathers itself,
consorts with wild irreducible Presence
and God/not God enters and leaves

Gnosis 2

What if a palm tree in Egypt bent down
to refresh a translucent babe
or he who ate figs in Nazareth
dined earlier as a god in Egypt?

Give us your names of unknowing
let the gathering begin;
for the One we all enter and leave
has fallen through a crack of dark.

Gnosis 3

Obscure and rare that state in which
falling I fell
or rose, no,
floated awake
into your invisible arms.

You whispered, Desirée,
and touched me with a thousand
exquisite fingers—
a rush like hummingbird wings

filtering through every parcel
from crown to toe to crown,
crescendo and fall, continuing
night's entire enterprise.

We flowed and spiralled in the shakras
of the spine, blossomed in the
thousand-petalled lotus of the brain.

You were not in and out and away
like any ordinary lover, but lingered
all night, sequestering, calling me
beloved

and I told no one when the morning rose.

On Blake's "The Lord Answering Job Out of the Whirlwind"

Younger and ever younger angels swirl
out of the rivering beard (indistinguishable
from the body) of that cruel, benign
patriarch plumed with outstretched
arms in a massive funnel or tunnelling
wind, blasting earth.

And underneath, crouched in adoration,
the shrouded form of Job, looking
in every way like a mirror
of his cruel and lovely God.

And further below in brown shadowy loops
the amorphous Comforters prostrate themselves.
Only Job's eyes pierce lightward,
fingers aghast, enamoured.

But the alien, nameless wife
who cursed that ghostly wind
is nowhere in the scene.

Holy, Holy, Holy

Why three holinesses? Earth, sky
and the whole that holds them in
one staggering breath. All is hale
hagiography somewhere, but here
"the broken rounds," said Browning.

And even in this wild geography
of snapped synapses, the mouth
forms its ahs before the pert
fullnesses of robins, and the
demented fullness of a woman

who pauses in her anxiety to
observe and listen to the most
high, most high, invading
her chatter, calming her dark
Lenten bones. Here in its knitting

She-Spirit weaves coverings,
hovers thrice holy.

"Lift Up Your Heads, O Gates
And Be Lifted Up, You Everlasting Doors"

Guardians of vital speech,
with ears honed, hearing first
the steps of the Holy
of golden oil-drenched feet and head,
hearing before seeing the naked
one who rides through, into you,
transforming your hinges' brass to gold.

Were you always carved in me,
swinging open in the small breath?

I Am Alpha and Omega

A to Z (whether you say zee or zed),
the alphabetical round, all sounds
holding hands to utter lament or praise

from the original river to the final
house of sea where delicate seahorses
rock sunward. What if every ending

really opens out and the skin tightens
and refills with elasticity, and
infant mouth opens to say o and o?

What if in one or two or three
the serpent rolls end to end so
head and tail are indistinguishable

and the creases fly away unknotted
from the brow, or a child steps out
of a pile of rotting flesh saying, "I Am Am Am

of renewal there is no end"?

**"The Temple of God Is Holy,
Which Temple, You Are"**
Habakkuk

How did the divine Geometer
find a place inside me, set up
a stool and begin sketching out
the divine proportions on my floor?

By what reversal did the house
of God invert itself, nature turn
inside out and proclaim
its kingdom here?

How in all this dark, rugged terrain
did someone light a single taper,
the endless canopy shrink itself
to such radical finitude?

And how does that unknowable
Presence host me to my kitchen,
run the vacuum, help prepare
and divide the next meal?

The Sacrifice of Thanksgiving

"And lily-coloured clothes provide
Your spouse not laboured-at nor spun."
  G.M. Hopkins

Is that all? all demanded?
when the heart is uncorked champagne,
effortless crack and spurt of evanescence,
an easeful "thanks" in a sacred space
you did not place or labour at?

Praise, praise that events fell
this way and not another;
praise inevitability that they fell
at all, and gladness, "your spouse
not laboured-at nor spun," the prize
re-prized, sweet reprisal:
return of a peace you did not make.

How remarkable that the wood-smoke rises
and the heart sleeps calmly on its bed

that this overflow is measured
somewhere as a giving.

Footbaths for Learners

Hands cup calloused, dust-enamelled feet,
hands sanded by carpentry's plane,

softened by psalm sheaves,
hardened by nocturnal fist's clinch.

Hands grasp the unbalanced ball of the foot
that has pressed earth's floor,

tenderly sweep over tarsus, metatarsus,
admiring the intricate, finicky bones,

easing in doomed palms
arches' stress and whine.

Blessed Are the Meek

if you mean the humbled
before starfish in starscape
blessed are the wildly dumbfounded
by robust organic wheels
that move us round
what star our centre moves

if you mean those who are inexpressibly happy
in lush peonies' breath, the waft
of mock orange wearing white shoulders

but not if you mean humble pie deference,
the predicted suburban round, smoothing
the edges of male ego's rub.

Let us be voiceless before honeybee's prelude
mouthed in roses,
not silenced by fear or diffidence.

Let us be mothers or not mothers
in our own ways and times.

Blessed are the lambs
for their union with grass and herb,
and cursed be the meekness that hides
and bends and quenches its own fire.

So ask us not,
the ravaged and defoliated,
to forgive our accusers and abusers
when it is they who need
that admonishment.

For blessed (not merely happy)
are the emptied

of what they thought themselves
for they shall inherit all
the lovely earthen things

that they are, and the sky as well.

Blessed Are the Merciful

"Vast floods of Mercy thrown on resistance."
Denise Levertov

For mercy I twist
as all must
if mercy and justice are one, long
for her light-teased face
all severing angles burned

when mercy drops myrrh from our palms
we are dropping clouds
and the mercy we dispense
shall be turned back
as rain or chute

Mercy in the bowels
mercy in the heart valves
mercy for the dogs and kids
mercy for the underemployed and overemployed
mercy for the pregnant teen
and the mercenary soldier

even if there is no mercy
yet I will have mercy on myself
for the crime of separateness

Blessed Are the Pure in Heart

whom no one sees or has seen
through knowing, thinking thoughts.

They shall not see a blaze of diaphanous light
or hollow bone in the desert turning

or a white rose burning
but a human face, eggshaped or heartshaped

slightly browned by the sun
pavement-weathered eyes softening

the look that plunges in and in
on the feather of a breath

the mercy that allows itself to be seen
by the blissed out, the open

Conch

The word is curved and round
like a roseate couch
where delicate, racy Aphrodite
might have reclined with Mars;
a seaflower for her quiet
stepping into the world;

an evolved and elongated ear
turned inside out
for the reception
of Siren's reedy song.

It is my daughter's pink bedroom
winding up into
a mysterious passage
to dark and darker pink,
so fleshy and pure
it will set her out gently
among the stars
that give but do not take
her small light.

Scars Don't Heal

and my heart-flow tears
cannot alter the brazen serpent's imprint
placed by a kettle's accidental fall
on your dearest fabric skin

which is you and not you, a veil.
Yet the bodies we built
when you studied in my womb
are unimpressed by outer coils.

A woman can carry the imprints of nails
in her hands and feet

and rise up sane.

Of darker inner scars may you remain free
O child of my flesh and bone.

Dancing at Long Beach

She fawn-steps and twirls
in fermenting light
mimicking some nimble-footed
mermaid's return from the sea.

Her hair is a sheath of amber
burning down her back.

She flings the fine sea mud,
pounds the turf with fierce wild toes.

Then all her seven years
bend to kiss the re-enchanted shore.

Called away
she finger traces, "I love you, sea,"
on clean canvas
repeating what her dance had already spoken.

Bridal Wreath Spirea

drifts like confetti
caresses the May Magnificat sky
decorates the earth with small white hands

ineluctable lyric air
in a suburban garden

variations in white unrevelling

clarifying into mist

Two Hearts Laid Bare

The crushed snail eyeballs
the opulent pink iris
laying herself out

just before she dies,
but not in time to inhale
her moony fragrance.

He withdraws his horn,
suitcases himself in dark
and gives himself birth.

Into and out of the dark
they weave their epiphanies.

Stand of Old Growth Beside the Highway: Easter Monday

As cushioning mosses receive your feet
and rain forest canopies tilt into your skin,
I spill myself in a thousand greens.

You rise from me—hemlock seedling
from cedar nurse log—soft strips of red
flaking down into the only sod.

Chickweed

Completely untoward,
serrated heartiness, raggedly
splashed across suburban turf,
undeterred by herbicides,
grappling with finer grasses

how they suggest outspoken
women who in middle-age declare
their free rights of passage

gripping down, tough-skinned,
inappropriate, uttering their solid
"life-is-not-a-golf-course" defiance.

Plutonian

In that Pluto region of the heart blue-
cold, waterless, unskied,
you are equivocal
and have no name, stand under no name
but ice, slanting your truth's
elliptical sway.

In that Plutonian cave
your postures clench,
unfold before mirrors and lakes
and layers of stripped sand.

There is a single note in all
that cold scale, a single reptilian
whistle on the bone;
and down that note you slide
into your own bathysphere gaze.

In the Bardos

In the dark and fusty bardos*
there is an odour
like that which permeates
the ceilings and floors
of aging institutions,

a dark incense,
earthbound fog
or smog teasing
its way indoors.

Not the odour of sanctity, not
the odour of death, though I
have hovered over dank
cities that emit it, and

watched its faces curl
over towers of learning,
sniffed it on my hands and knees
cleaning closets.

Only the pierce of lavender
or the subtle insinuation of jasmine
can cleanse it from the air.

*bardos - regions of the Tibetan underworld

You Ground Me in California

I am trillions of uncountable wires
criss-crossing into the ozone.

Channelled through you
they light a house.

I am gesticulating
about the Tibetan bardo-states

when you point to an orange tree
I might have stumbled over without seeing.

I am in a cloister eating fruit
and reading Jung.

You haul me out to feel the stretch of my legs,
toss my dreams across a sienna sky.

We are moving through wide-scented catalpas,
touching seedpods that crackle like words

in the poem that wouldn't have come without you.

From a Galilean Poet

The wind blows in
wherever there's an opening for it,
and you haven't got a clue where
it comes from or where it's heading.

Don't be surprised if I say you've
got to be born into that wind-world.
Call it above, or call it within;
imagine there's a cave you're crawling out.

And the wind-born will be twice born
but not from belief or theology,
an emotional trip or something
to stick on your bumper.

For God's sake, we're talking life,
we're talking poetry, slogan
larger moving through
that sings in the veins.

Veil, Unveil, Revel for the Bride

The veil lifts from earth
like dew condensed, rises, drifts
back down in airy folds over everything—

cities, towns, countrysides, high rises, maps,
antique Queen Anne's lace; fresh
as hyacinth or lily-of-the-valley

coating and covering all harsh lines
and edges of doors and windows; unyellowed,
soft, vestal, glowing slightly.

Falls, covers, shields, filters, kisses,
is light, almost diaphanous, unstifling
all it clothes. Most breathe it unawares.

Rainbows rumour through its intricate
weave; silken angels, gentle spiders
with enormous eyes shake it out,

fine linen from the four corners
rippling across space. "The Bride's lace."
From Bride to bride, a shining gift,

enormous white jelly-fish with sails
billowing, floating, hushed, over all.